Dolphins Twist and Spin

Written by Michèle Dufresne

PIONEER VALLEY EDUCATIONAL PRESS, INC.

Look at the **dolphin**.
Dolphins can swim fast.

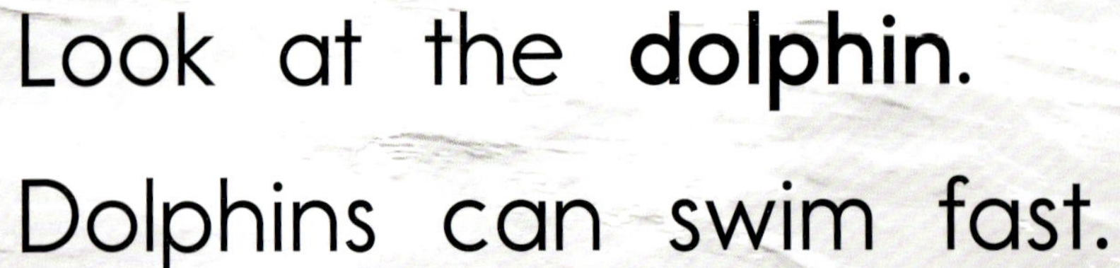

Dolphins are marine mammals. They live in all the seas and oceans and even in some rivers around the world.

Can you see the dolphins?
The dolphins blend into
the **water**.

Dolphins use countershading to blend into their surroundings. They have dark backs, making them hard to see from above. They also have light bellies that blend with the surface of the water when seen from below.

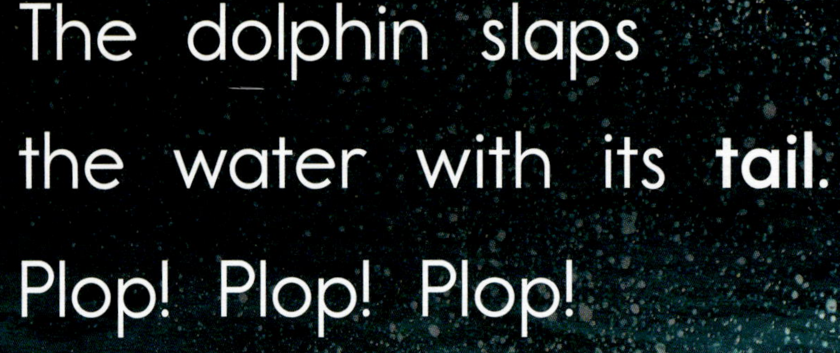

The dolphin slaps
the water with its **tail.**
Plop! Plop! Plop!

Dolphins slap the water to get the attention of other dolphins and to warn them of danger.

Click! Click! Click!

Dolphins make clicking sounds, whistles, and squeals to communicate with other dolphins.

The dolphin pumps its tail
and jumps out
of the water.
Look at it twist
and spin!

8

Spinner dolphins are well-known for their acrobatic spins.

Oh no!
Can we help the
baby dolphin?
It is stuck in a net.

Sometimes dolphins get tangled in fishing nets. They also swallow plastic that's floating in the ocean, thinking it is food.

glossary